Table of Contents

Chapter 1: Introduction to AI Trends and Insights

Evolution of AI Research

Over the years, the field of artificial intelligence (AI) research has evolved significantly, driven by advancements in technology and increasing demand for intelligent systems across various industries. The evolution of AI research can be traced back to the 1950s, when scientists first began exploring the concept of artificial intelligence and its potential applications. Since then, AI research has made tremendous progress, with researchers developing increasingly sophisticated algorithms and techniques to mimic human intelligence.

In the United States, AI research has been at the forefront of technological advancements, with leading institutions such as Stanford University, MIT, and Google's DeepMind leading the way in developing cutting-edge AI technologies. The US government has also invested heavily in AI research, recognizing its potential to drive economic growth and innovation. As a result, the US remains a global leader in AI research and development, attracting top talent and investment from around the world.

In China, AI research has also seen rapid growth in recent years, fueled by government support and a growing ecosystem of startups and tech companies. Chinese researchers have made significant contributions to AI, particularly in the fields of machine learning and natural language processing. With large amounts of data and a highly skilled workforce, China has become a key player in the global AI landscape, competing with the US for dominance in the field.

In the United Kingdom, AI research has been driven by a strong academic community and a thriving startup ecosystem. Leading universities such as Oxford and Cambridge have been at the forefront of AI research, producing groundbreaking research in areas such as computer vision and robotics. The UK government has also recognized the importance of AI, investing in initiatives to promote AI research and innovation across various industries.

In Israel, Canada, France, India, Japan, Germany, and Singapore, AI research has also grown significantly in recent years, with each country making unique contributions to the field. From developing AI-powered healthcare solutions in Israel to advancing autonomous driving technology in Germany, these countries are playing an increasingly important role in shaping the future of AI. As AI continues to evolve, it is clear that global collaboration and knowledge sharing will be crucial in driving further advancements in the field.

Importance of AI Investment

In today's rapidly evolving technological landscape, artificial intelligence (AI) has emerged as a key driver of innovation and growth across various industries. As such, the importance of investing in AI research and development cannot be overstated. With countries like the United States, China, United Kingdom, Israel, Canada, France, India, Japan, Germany, and Singapore leading the charge in AI investment and technological advancements, it is crucial for stakeholders in these regions to understand the significance of prioritizing AI investment.

One of the primary reasons for the importance of AI investment is the potential for significant economic returns. AI technologies have the capability to streamline processes, enhance productivity, and drive revenue growth for businesses. By investing in AI research and development, countries can position themselves at the forefront of the global AI market, gaining a competitive edge and reaping the benefits of early adoption. This is particularly important for countries looking to solidify their position as leaders in technological innovation.

Furthermore, AI investment plays a crucial role in driving societal progress and addressing complex challenges. From healthcare and education to transportation and cybersecurity, AI technologies have the potential to revolutionize various aspects of our daily lives. By investing in AI research, countries can harness the power of AI to improve public services, enhance quality of life, and promote sustainable development. This underscores the importance of fostering a supportive ecosystem for AI investment, encompassing both public and private sector initiatives.

In addition to economic and societal benefits, AI investment also holds the key to unlocking new opportunities for collaboration and knowledge exchange. By investing in AI research and development, countries can foster partnerships with leading AI experts, institutions, and organizations around the world. This not only accelerates the pace of technological advancements but also promotes cross-border innovation and knowledge sharing. In an increasingly interconnected world, collaboration in AI investment is essential for driving global progress and ensuring the responsible development of AI technologies.

In conclusion, the importance of AI investment cannot be overstated in the context of today's rapidly evolving technological landscape. As countries like the United States, China, United Kingdom, Israel, Canada, France, India, Japan, Germany, and Singapore continue to lead the charge in AI research, investment, and technological advancements, it is essential for stakeholders in these regions to recognize the value of prioritizing AI investment. By investing in AI research and development, countries can unlock economic opportunities, drive societal progress, and foster collaboration on a global scale. Ultimately, AI investment is not just a strategic imperative but a cornerstone for building a sustainable future driven by innovation, growth, and prosperity.

Technological Advancements in AI

Technological advancements in AI have been rapidly evolving in recent years, with countries around the globe investing heavily in research and development to stay at the forefront of this field. The United States, China, United Kingdom, Israel, Canada, France, India, Japan, Germany, and Singapore are among the leading countries in AI research, investment, and technological advancements. These countries are not only competing with each other but also collaborating on various projects to push the boundaries of what AI can achieve.

In the United States, tech giants like Google, Amazon, and Microsoft are leading the way in AI research and development. The country's strong academic institutions and robust funding from both the government and private sector have helped propel the US to the forefront of AI innovation. China, on the other hand, has made significant strides in AI technology, with companies like Baidu, Alibaba, and Tencent investing heavily in AI research and development. The Chinese government has also outlined ambitious plans to become the global leader in AI by 2030.

The United Kingdom, Israel, Canada, France, India, Japan, Germany, and Singapore are also making significant contributions to the field of AI. The UK's strong research institutions and government support have positioned it as a key player in AI innovation. Israel is known for its thriving startup ecosystem, with many AI startups gaining international recognition for their groundbreaking technologies. Canada has also emerged as a leader in AI research, with its strong academic institutions and government support attracting top talent from around the world.

France, India, Japan, Germany, and Singapore are also investing heavily in AI research and development, with each country focusing on different areas of AI innovation. France is known for its expertise in natural language processing and robotics, while India is focusing on AI applications in healthcare and agriculture. Japan is at the forefront of AI robotics, with companies like Toyota and Softbank leading the way in developing AI-powered robots. Germany is known for its strong industrial base, with a focus on AI applications in manufacturing and logistics. Singapore, with its strong government support and focus on AI ethics, is positioning itself as a hub for AI research and development in Southeast Asia.

Overall, the future of AI looks bright, with countries around the globe making significant advancements in this field. By collaborating and sharing knowledge, these countries can continue to push the boundaries of what AI can achieve, leading to a future where AI technologies have a profound impact on society and the economy.

Chapter 2: United States

Overview of AI Research in the United States

The United States is a global leader in AI research, investment, and technological advancements. With a rich history of innovation and a robust ecosystem of universities, research institutions, and tech companies, the U.S. has been at the forefront of AI development for decades. From pioneering work in machine learning and neural networks to cutting-edge applications in autonomous vehicles and natural language processing, American researchers and entrepreneurs have been driving the evolution of AI technologies.

One of the key strengths of the U.S. AI ecosystem is its collaborative and interdisciplinary nature. Researchers from a wide range of disciplines – including computer science, mathematics, cognitive science, and neuroscience – work together to push the boundaries of what is possible with AI. This cross-pollination of ideas and expertise has led to breakthroughs in areas such as deep learning, reinforcement learning, and computer vision.

In addition to its academic and research institutions, the U.S. is home to a vibrant community of AI startups and venture capital firms. Silicon Valley, in particular, has become a hub for AI innovation, attracting top talent from around the world and serving as a launchpad for cutting-edge technologies. From self-driving cars to personalized healthcare solutions, American startups are pushing the envelope of what AI can achieve in a wide range of industries.

Despite its leadership in AI research and investment, the U.S. faces challenges in maintaining its competitive edge in the global AI landscape. With the rise of AI superpowers such as China and the European Union, American policymakers and industry leaders are grappling with issues such as talent retention, data privacy, and ethical AI development. In order to stay ahead of the curve, the U.S. will need to continue investing in research, fostering collaboration between academia and industry, and addressing the societal implications of AI technologies.

Overall, the future of AI in the United States looks bright. With a strong foundation of research excellence, a dynamic entrepreneurial ecosystem, and a culture of innovation, the U.S. is well-positioned to lead the next wave of AI breakthroughs. By building on its strengths and addressing its challenges, America can continue to shape the future of AI for the benefit of society and the economy.

Leading AI Companies in the United States

In recent years, the United States has emerged as a global leader in artificial intelligence (AI) research, investment, and technological advancements. The country is home to some of the most innovative and forward-thinking AI companies in the world, driving the development of cutting-edge technologies that are shaping the future of industries across the board. In this subchapter, we will take a closer look at some of the leading AI companies in the United States, their contributions to the field, and the impact they are having on the global AI landscape.

One of the most prominent AI companies in the United States is Google, a subsidiary of Alphabet Inc. Google has been at the forefront of AI research and development for years, leveraging its vast resources and talent pool to push the boundaries of what is possible with artificial intelligence. From self-driving cars to natural language processing, Google's AI initiatives span a wide range of applications and have had a significant impact on the way we interact with technology.

Another key player in the US AI scene is Microsoft, which has invested heavily in AI research and development through its Microsoft Research division. The company has made significant strides in areas such as machine learning, computer vision, and natural language understanding, and its AI technologies are being integrated into a wide range of products and services, from cloud computing to productivity tools.

In the realm of healthcare AI, companies like IBM Watson Health are leading the charge in using artificial intelligence to revolutionize the way we approach medical diagnostics, treatment planning, and personalized medicine. IBM's AI-powered solutions are helping healthcare providers deliver more accurate and efficient care, ultimately improving patient outcomes and reducing costs.

On the startup front, companies like OpenAI and DeepMind are pushing the boundaries of AI research with their cutting-edge algorithms and groundbreaking applications. These companies are attracting top talent from around the world and are shaping the future of AI in areas such as reinforcement learning, robotics, and natural language processing.

Overall, the United States continues to be a powerhouse in the global AI landscape, with its leading companies driving innovation and pushing the boundaries of what is possible with artificial intelligence. As the field continues to evolve, these companies will play a crucial role in shaping the future of AI research, investment, and technological advancements not only in the US but also around the globe.

Government Initiatives in AI

Governments around the world are increasingly recognizing the importance of artificial intelligence (AI) and are taking steps to support research, investment, and technological advancements in this field. In the United States, the government has launched several initiatives to promote AI innovation, including the National Artificial Intelligence Research and Development Strategic Plan. This plan outlines the government's commitment to advancing AI research and development in areas such as healthcare, transportation, and national security.

In China, the government has made AI a top priority in its national development plans. The Chinese government has pledged billions of dollars in funding for AI research and development, and has set ambitious targets for becoming a global leader in AI by 2030. Initiatives such as the New Generation Artificial Intelligence Development Plan aim to support the growth of China's AI industry and foster collaboration between government, industry, and academia.

In the United Kingdom, the government has established the AI Sector Deal, which aims to boost the country's AI capabilities and drive economic growth. The government has also launched the Office for Artificial Intelligence to coordinate AI policy and strategy across government departments. These initiatives are designed to support the growth of the UK's AI sector and ensure that the country remains at the forefront of AI innovation.

In Israel, the government has launched the National Artificial Intelligence Initiative to support research and development in AI across academia, industry, and government. The initiative aims to position Israel as a global leader in AI and to drive economic growth through the adoption of AI technologies. The government has also established the National Council for Artificial Intelligence to oversee the implementation of AI policy and strategy.

In Canada, the government has launched the Pan-Canadian Artificial Intelligence Strategy to support research and innovation in AI. The strategy aims to position Canada as a world leader in AI and to drive economic growth through the development and adoption of AI technologies. Initiatives such as the Vector Institute for Artificial Intelligence and the Canadian Institute for Advanced Research are helping to support AI research and talent development in Canada.

Future Trends in AI in the United States

The future of AI in the United States is one that is filled with promise and potential. As one of the leading countries in AI research, investment, and technological advancements, the US is poised to continue driving innovation in this field for years to come. With a strong foundation in academia, industry, and government support, the US is well-positioned to stay at the forefront of AI development.

One of the key trends that we can expect to see in the future of AI in the United States is the continued growth of AI applications in various industries. From healthcare to finance to transportation, AI is being increasingly used to improve efficiency, accuracy, and decision-making processes. As more companies and organizations in the US adopt AI technologies, we can expect to see a proliferation of new and innovative applications that will transform the way we live and work.

Another trend that we can expect to see in the future of AI in the United States is the increasing focus on ethics and regulation. As AI technologies become more advanced and pervasive, there is a growing recognition of the need to ensure that these technologies are developed and used responsibly. This includes addressing issues such as bias, privacy, and accountability, as well as developing frameworks for ethical AI development and deployment.

In addition, we can expect to see continued collaboration and competition in the field of AI among the United States and other leading countries such as China, the United Kingdom, Israel, Canada, France, India, Japan, Germany, and Singapore. As AI becomes an increasingly global phenomenon, countries around the world are working together to share knowledge, resources, and expertise in order to advance the field. At the same time, there is also healthy competition among these countries to be the leaders in AI research and innovation.

Overall, the future of AI in the United States looks bright. With a strong foundation in research, investment, and technological advancements, the US is well-positioned to continue driving innovation in this field. By staying at the forefront of AI development, addressing ethical and regulatory challenges, and collaborating with other leading countries, the US can continue to lead the way in shaping the future of AI for the benefit of society as a whole.

Chapter 3: China

Growth of AI Industry in China

In recent years, China has emerged as a global leader in the field of artificial intelligence (AI), experiencing rapid growth and development in the industry. The country has made significant investments in AI research, attracting top talent and fostering innovation in the sector. With a combination of government support, strong academic institutions, and a thriving tech industry, China has positioned itself as a powerhouse in the AI industry.

One of the key factors contributing to the growth of the AI industry in China is the government's commitment to promoting technological advancements. The Chinese government has implemented policies and initiatives aimed at supporting AI research and development, providing funding and resources to companies and institutions working in the field. This support has helped to create a favorable environment for AI innovation, attracting both domestic and international investment in the sector.

China's tech industry is another driving force behind the growth of the AI industry in the country. With companies like Baidu, Alibaba, and Tencent leading the way in AI research and development, China has become a hub for cutting-edge technology and innovation. These companies are investing heavily in AI technologies, developing new applications and solutions that are shaping the future of the industry.

In addition to government support and a strong tech industry, China boasts a wealth of talent in the field of AI. The country is home to some of the world's top AI researchers and experts, who are driving innovation and pushing the boundaries of what is possible in the field. With a growing number of AI startups and research institutions, China is well-positioned to continue its leadership in the global AI industry.

Overall, the growth of the AI industry in China presents exciting opportunities for collaboration and partnership with other countries and regions around the world. As China continues to invest in AI research, innovation, and technological advancements, the country is poised to play a key role in shaping the future of AI on a global scale. AI research, investment, and technological advancements in United States, China, United Kingdom, Israel, Canada, France, India, Japan,

Germany, and Singapore can benefit from the advancements and expertise coming out of China's thriving AI industry.

Key Players in Chinese AI Market

In the rapidly evolving landscape of artificial intelligence (AI), China has emerged as a key player with significant investments and advancements in the field. Several major companies and institutions in China are leading the charge in AI research, development, and innovation. Understanding the key players in the Chinese AI market is crucial for anyone looking to stay informed and competitive in this dynamic industry.

One of the most prominent players in the Chinese AI market is Baidu, often referred to as the "Google of China." Baidu has made significant investments in AI research and development, particularly in the areas of natural language processing, image recognition, and autonomous driving. The company's AI-powered products and services have gained widespread adoption in China and beyond, solidifying its position as a leader in the field.

Another major player in the Chinese AI market is Tencent, a leading technology company known for its popular messaging app WeChat. Tencent has been investing heavily in AI technologies, with a focus on applications such as gaming, social media, and e-commerce. The company's AI research lab is at the forefront of cutting-edge developments in machine learning, computer vision, and speech recognition.

Alibaba, the e-commerce giant, is also a key player in the Chinese AI market. Alibaba's AI research institute, known as the DAMO Academy, focuses on a wide range of AI technologies, including cloud computing, robotics, and natural language processing. The company's AI-powered platforms and services have transformed various industries, from retail and finance to healthcare and logistics.

In addition to these tech giants, Chinese universities and research institutions are also making significant contributions to the country's AI ecosystem. Institutes such as Tsinghua University, Peking University, and the Chinese Academy of Sciences are conducting cutting-edge research in AI and collaborating with industry partners to drive technological advancements. These academic institutions play a crucial role in shaping the future of AI in China and beyond.

Overall, the key players in the Chinese AI market are driving innovation, research, and investment in the field, positioning the country as a global leader in artificial intelligence. As AI continues to revolutionize industries and societies worldwide, keeping a close eye on these players and their developments will be essential for anyone involved in AI research, investment, and technological advancements across the globe.

Government Policies Supporting AI Development

As artificial intelligence (AI) continues to revolutionize various industries and sectors, governments around the world are recognizing the importance of supporting AI development through strategic policies and initiatives. In this subchapter, we will explore the government policies that are driving AI research, investment, and technological advancements in countries such as the United States, China, United Kingdom, Israel, Canada, France, India, Japan, Germany, and Singapore.

In the United States, the government has taken a proactive approach to supporting AI development through initiatives such as the National Artificial Intelligence Research and Development Strategic Plan. This plan outlines the government's commitment to investing in AI research and development to maintain the country's leadership in AI innovation. Additionally, the U.S. government has established the Select Committee on Artificial Intelligence to provide recommendations on AI policy and regulation.

In China, the government has made AI a national priority through initiatives such as the New Generation Artificial Intelligence Development Plan. This plan aims to make China the world leader in AI innovation by 2030 through investments in research and development, talent development, and infrastructure. The Chinese government has also implemented policies to support AI startups and encourage collaboration between industry and academia.

In the United Kingdom, the government has launched the AI Sector Deal to drive growth and innovation in the AI industry. This deal includes investments in AI research and development, funding for AI startups, and initiatives to develop AI talent. The UK government has also established the Office for Artificial Intelligence to oversee the implementation of AI policies and support the growth of the AI sector.

In Israel, the government has established the Israel Innovation Authority to support AI research and development through funding and grants. The government has also launched initiatives such as the National AI Program to promote collaboration between industry, academia, and government agencies. Israel's strong focus on AI has led to the country becoming a global hub for AI innovation and startups.

In Canada, the government has developed the Pan-Canadian Artificial Intelligence Strategy to support AI research and development across the country. This strategy includes investments in AI research, funding for AI startups, and initiatives to develop AI talent. The Canadian government has also established the Canadian Institute for Advanced Research to support interdisciplinary AI research and collaboration.

Challenges and Opportunities in Chinese AI Sector

The Chinese AI sector is currently facing a series of unique challenges and opportunities that are shaping the future of the industry in the country. One of the main challenges facing the Chinese AI sector is the intense competition from other global players, particularly in the United States. With companies like Google, Facebook, and Amazon leading the way in AI research and development, Chinese companies are finding it increasingly difficult to keep up with the pace of innovation and technological advancements.

However, despite these challenges, there are also numerous opportunities for growth and expansion in the Chinese AI sector. One of the key opportunities lies in the massive market potential in China, with its large population and growing middle class creating a huge demand for AI-powered products and services. Additionally, the Chinese government has been actively supporting the development of AI technology in the country through initiatives such as the "Made in China 2025" plan, which aims to make China a global leader in AI by 2025.

Another major opportunity for the Chinese AI sector is the abundance of data available in the country. With over 800 million internet users and a rapidly digitizing economy, China has access to vast amounts of data that can be used to train AI algorithms and improve the performance of AI systems. This data advantage has already helped Chinese companies like Baidu, Alibaba, and Tencent to become leaders in AI research and development.

In order to capitalize on these opportunities and overcome the challenges facing the Chinese AI sector, it is crucial for companies and researchers in China to collaborate with their counterparts in other countries. By sharing knowledge, resources, and expertise, AI professionals from around the globe can work together to drive innovation and advancement in the field. This collaboration will not only benefit the Chinese AI sector but also contribute to the growth and development of AI technology on a global scale.

Overall, the Chinese AI sector is at a critical juncture, facing both challenges and opportunities that will shape its future trajectory. By leveraging its market potential, data advantage, and government support, China has the potential to become a global leader in AI research, investment, and technological advancements. With collaboration and cooperation between AI professionals from different countries, the Chinese AI sector can overcome its challenges and emerge as a key player in the global AI landscape.

Chapter 4: United Kingdom

AI Research Landscape in the United Kingdom

The United Kingdom has long been a hub for cutting-edge research and innovation in the field of artificial intelligence (AI). With a rich history of scientific discovery and a strong tradition of academic excellence, the UK is home to some of the world's leading AI researchers and institutions. In recent years, the country has made significant investments in AI research, leading to the development of groundbreaking technologies and the emergence of new opportunities for collaboration and growth.

One of the key strengths of the UK's AI research landscape is its diverse and vibrant ecosystem of academic institutions, startups, and multinational corporations. Leading universities such as Oxford, Cambridge, and Imperial College London have established world-class research centers focused on AI and machine learning, attracting top talent from around the globe. In addition, the UK government has launched several initiatives to support AI research and development, including the establishment of the UK Research and Innovation agency and the creation of the Industrial Strategy Challenge Fund.

The UK is also home to a thriving AI startup scene, with London emerging as a major hub for innovation and entrepreneurship in the field. The city's vibrant tech ecosystem has attracted a growing number of AI startups, many of which are pioneering new technologies and applications in areas such as healthcare, finance, and cybersecurity. In addition, the UK government has introduced a range of incentives and programs to support AI startups, including tax breaks, funding opportunities, and access to mentorship and networking resources.

In terms of technological advancements, the UK has made significant progress in areas such as natural language processing, computer vision, and reinforcement learning. Researchers at institutions such as DeepMind, the University of Edinburgh, and the Alan Turing Institute have made important contributions to the development of AI technologies that are reshaping industries and transforming society. In addition, the UK government has prioritized AI as a key driver of economic growth and competitiveness, investing in initiatives to promote the responsible and ethical use of AI technologies.

Overall, the UK's AI research landscape is characterized by a strong foundation of scientific excellence, a culture of innovation and collaboration, and a commitment to using AI for the benefit of society. As the country continues to invest in AI research and development, it is well positioned to play a leading role in shaping the future of AI on a global scale. By fostering partnerships with other key players in the AI ecosystem, the UK can leverage its strengths in research, investment, and technological advancements to drive forward the next wave of AI innovation and create new opportunities for growth and prosperity.

AI Startups in the UK

AI startups in the UK have been gaining significant attention and traction in recent years. The UK has established itself as a hub for AI innovation, with a growing number of startups emerging in various sectors such as healthcare, finance, and cybersecurity. These startups are leveraging cutting-edge technologies and algorithms to develop innovative solutions that are revolutionizing industries and driving economic growth.

One of the key factors contributing to the success of AI startups in the UK is the strong support from the government and the availability of funding and resources. The UK government has been actively promoting AI research and development through initiatives such as the AI Sector Deal and the Industrial Strategy Challenge Fund. This has created a conducive environment for startups to thrive and attract investment from both domestic and international sources.

In addition to government support, the UK also boasts a thriving ecosystem of universities, research institutions, and accelerators that provide startups with access to top talent, expertise, and mentorship. This has enabled AI startups in the UK to develop cutting-edge technologies and products that are competitive on a global scale. Furthermore, the presence of major tech companies and multinational corporations in the UK has created opportunities for startups to collaborate, partner, and scale their businesses.

AI startups in the UK are also benefiting from the country's strong legal and regulatory framework, which provides a level playing field for startups to operate and grow. The UK has been at the forefront of developing ethical guidelines and regulations for AI technologies, ensuring that startups adhere to best practices and uphold high standards of data privacy and security. This has helped build trust and credibility among customers and investors, paving the way for the continued growth and success of AI startups in the UK.

Overall, the future looks bright for AI startups in the UK as they continue to push the boundaries of innovation and drive technological advancements across industries. With the right support, resources, and a talented pool of entrepreneurs and researchers, the UK is poised to remain a global leader in AI research, investment, and technological advancements for years to come.

Collaboration between Academia and Industry in AI

Collaboration between academia and industry in the field of artificial intelligence (AI) is crucial for driving innovation and pushing the boundaries of what is possible. In the United States, renowned universities such as Stanford, MIT, and Carnegie Mellon have established strong partnerships with industry giants like Google, Facebook, and Microsoft. These collaborations not only facilitate the transfer of knowledge and expertise but also lead to the development of cutting-edge technologies that have the potential to revolutionize the way we live and work.

In China, the government has been actively promoting collaboration between academia and industry in AI research and development. Companies like Baidu, Alibaba, and Tencent have invested heavily in partnerships with universities to leverage their research capabilities and drive innovation in areas such as natural language processing, computer vision, and autonomous driving. This close collaboration has helped China become a global leader in AI technology and is positioning the country to shape the future of AI on a global scale.

In the United Kingdom, academic institutions such as Oxford, Cambridge, and Imperial College London have established strong ties with industry players like DeepMind, ARM, and British Telecom. These partnerships have led to significant advancements in AI research and have resulted in the creation of spin-off companies that are commercializing cutting-edge AI technologies. The UK government has also been supportive of these collaborations, providing funding and incentives to encourage further innovation in the field.

In Israel, the collaboration between academia and industry in AI has been instrumental in driving the country's reputation as a global hub for innovation. Companies like Mobileye, Waze, and OrCam have emerged from partnerships with academic institutions such as the Technion and Hebrew University, leading to breakthroughs in areas like computer vision, robotics, and natural language processing. This collaboration has not only put Israel on the map as a leader in AI technology but has also attracted significant investment from international players looking to tap into the country's expertise in the field.

In Canada, France, India, Japan, Germany, and Singapore, similar trends can be observed in the collaboration between academia and industry in AI research and development. Companies in these countries are partnering with universities to access top talent and cutting-edge research, while academic institutions are benefiting from industry funding and resources to drive their research forward. These collaborations are essential for fostering innovation, accelerating the development of AI technologies, and ensuring that these countries remain competitive in the global AI landscape.

Regulatory Framework for AI in the UK

The regulatory framework for AI in the UK is a crucial aspect that AI research, investment, and technological advancements in the country need to consider. The UK government has recognized the importance of regulating AI technologies to ensure their safe and ethical use. As such, there are several laws and guidelines in place to govern the development and deployment of AI systems in the UK.

One of the key pieces of legislation in the UK regarding AI is the Data Protection Act 2018, which incorporates the EU's General Data Protection Regulation (GDPR). This legislation sets out rules for the collection, processing, and storage of personal data, which is particularly important in the context of AI systems that rely on large amounts of data to operate effectively. Compliance with data protection regulations is essential for AI companies operating in the UK.

In addition to data protection laws, the UK government has also published guidelines for the ethical use of AI. The AI Code of Conduct, developed by the UK's Department for Digital, Culture, Media and Sport, sets out principles for the responsible use of AI technologies. These principles include transparency, accountability, fairness, and privacy, and are intended to guide AI developers and users in ensuring that their systems are ethical and compliant with legal requirements.

The UK's regulatory framework for AI also includes the establishment of the Centre for Data Ethics and Innovation (CDEI). The CDEI is an independent advisory body that advises the government on the ethical and regulatory implications of AI and data-driven technologies. The CDEI works with industry, academia, and civil society to develop best practices and guidelines for the responsible use of AI in the UK.

Overall, the regulatory framework for AI in the UK is designed to promote innovation while ensuring that AI technologies are developed and deployed in a safe, ethical, and responsible manner. By adhering to data protection laws, ethical guidelines, and working with organizations like the CDEI, AI research, investment, and technological advancements in the UK can thrive while protecting individuals' rights and promoting public trust in AI systems.

Chapter 5: Israel

Innovation in AI from Israel

Israel has emerged as a leading hub for innovation in the field of artificial intelligence (AI), attracting attention from researchers, investors, and tech enthusiasts from around the globe. With a strong emphasis on innovation and entrepreneurship, Israel has become a hotbed for cutting-edge AI technologies that are shaping the future of various industries.

One of the key factors driving Israel's success in AI is its vibrant ecosystem of startups and research institutions that are pushing the boundaries of what is possible with AI. Companies like Mobileye, a pioneer in autonomous driving technology, and Deep Instinct, a cybersecurity firm using AI to detect and prevent cyber threats, are just a few examples of the innovative AI companies that have emerged from Israel.

Israel's strong ties to the United States, China, and other leading AI hubs have also played a significant role in its rise as a global AI powerhouse. Israeli startups often collaborate with international partners to access new markets, funding, and expertise, helping them accelerate their growth and impact on the global stage.

Furthermore, Israel's emphasis on investing in AI research and development has led to the creation of world-class research institutions and academic programs that are producing top talent in the field of AI. This talent pool, combined with the country's entrepreneurial spirit and supportive government policies, has created a fertile ground for AI innovation to thrive in Israel.

As AI continues to revolutionize industries and transform the way we live and work, Israel's contributions to the field are likely to play a significant role in shaping the future of AI on a global scale. With its unique blend of innovation, collaboration, and talent, Israel is poised to continue pushing the boundaries of what is possible with AI, driving advancements that will benefit not only the country itself but also the wider global community.

Israeli AI Startups Making Waves

In recent years, Israeli AI startups have been making waves in the global tech scene. Known for their innovation and cutting-edge technology, these startups are attracting attention from investors and tech giants alike. With a strong focus on AI research, investment, and technological advancements, Israel has become a hub for AI innovation.

One of the key factors driving the success of Israeli AI startups is the country's world-class talent pool. Israel is home to some of the brightest minds in the tech industry, many of whom have a background in AI research. This talent pool has helped Israeli startups develop groundbreaking AI technologies that are revolutionizing industries around the world.

Israeli AI startups are also known for their strong focus on collaboration and partnerships. Many of these startups work closely with universities, research institutions, and other tech companies to drive innovation and bring their products to market. This collaborative approach has helped Israeli startups stay at the forefront of the AI industry and continue to push the boundaries of what is possible with AI technology.

In addition to their focus on research and collaboration, Israeli AI startups are also attracting significant investment from both local and international investors. With a track record of success and a reputation for developing cutting-edge technologies, Israeli AI startups are seen as a smart investment for those looking to get in on the ground floor of the next big thing in tech.

Overall, Israeli AI startups are leading the way in the global AI industry, with their innovative technologies and collaborative approach setting them apart from the competition. As the AI industry continues to grow and evolve, it is clear that Israeli startups will play a key role in shaping the future of AI technology.

Government Support for AI Innovation in Israel

Israel has emerged as a global hub for AI innovation, with the government playing a crucial role in supporting the growth of the industry. Through various initiatives and programs, the Israeli government has been instrumental in fostering a thriving ecosystem for AI research, investment, and technological advancements in the country.

One of the key ways in which the Israeli government supports AI innovation is through funding and grants. The government provides financial support to AI startups and companies through programs such as the Israel Innovation Authority (IIA) and the Office of the Chief Scientist (OCS). These programs offer grants, loans, and other forms of financial assistance to help AI companies develop and commercialize their technologies.

In addition to financial support, the Israeli government also invests in infrastructure and resources to support AI innovation. For example, the government has established several AI research centers and institutes, such as the Technion-Israel Institute of Technology and the Weizmann Institute of Science, which provide cutting-edge facilities and resources for AI researchers and entrepreneurs.

Furthermore, the Israeli government actively promotes collaboration and partnerships between industry, academia, and government agencies to drive AI innovation. Through initiatives such as the National AI Initiative and the Israel Innovation Network, the government facilitates collaboration between different stakeholders in the AI ecosystem, fostering a culture of innovation and knowledge-sharing.

Overall, the government's support for AI innovation in Israel has been instrumental in establishing the country as a global leader in the field. By providing funding, resources, and fostering collaboration, the Israeli government has created a fertile ground for AI research, investment, and technological advancements, attracting top talent and companies from around the world to contribute to the country's vibrant AI ecosystem.

Israel's Position in the Global AI Market

Israel has emerged as a significant player in the global AI market, with a thriving ecosystem of startups, research institutions, and multinational companies contributing to its rapid growth. With a strong focus on innovation and technological advancements, Israel has become a hub for AI research, investment, and development.

One of the key factors driving Israel's success in the AI market is its highly skilled workforce. The country boasts a strong education system that produces a steady stream of talented engineers, data scientists, and AI experts. In addition, Israel's military service has played a crucial role in cultivating a culture of innovation and problem-solving, which has translated into the development of cutting-edge AI technologies.

Israel is also known for its vibrant startup ecosystem, with thousands of tech companies, many of which are focused on AI. These startups benefit from a supportive environment that includes government grants, access to venture capital, and collaboration opportunities with multinational corporations. As a result, Israel has produced a number of successful AI startups that have attracted international attention and investment.

Furthermore, Israel's strategic location at the crossroads of Europe, Asia, and Africa has positioned it as a gateway to the global AI market. The country's proximity to major markets such as the United States and Europe, as well as its strong ties with countries in the Middle East and Asia, make it an attractive destination for multinational companies looking to establish a presence in the region.

Overall, Israel's position in the global AI market is a testament to its commitment to innovation, entrepreneurship, and collaboration. With a strong foundation in research, investment, and technological advancements, Israel is well-positioned to continue driving the future of AI on a global scale.

Chapter 6: Canada

AI Ecosystem in Canada

Canada has emerged as a key player in the global AI ecosystem, with a rapidly growing community of researchers, entrepreneurs, and investors dedicated to advancing artificial intelligence technologies. The country is home to several world-class research institutions, such as the Vector Institute for Artificial Intelligence and the Montreal Institute for Learning Algorithms (MILA), which are at the forefront of AI research and innovation.

One of the key strengths of Canada's AI ecosystem is its collaborative and interdisciplinary approach to research and development. The country's universities, research institutions, and industry partners work closely together to foster innovation and drive the adoption of AI technologies across various sectors, including healthcare, finance, and transportation. This collaborative spirit has helped Canada attract top talent from around the world and establish itself as a hub for cutting-edge AI research.

In addition to its strong research community, Canada also boasts a vibrant startup ecosystem that is fueling the growth of AI companies in the country. Toronto, Montreal, and Vancouver are home to a growing number of AI startups that are developing innovative solutions in areas such as computer vision, natural language processing, and robotics. These startups are attracting significant investments from both domestic and international investors, further cementing Canada's position as a global leader in AI innovation.

Moreover, the Canadian government has been proactive in supporting the development of AI technologies in the country. In 2017, the government launched the Pan-Canadian Artificial Intelligence Strategy, which included an investment of over $125 million to support AI research and talent development. This funding has helped Canada attract top researchers and entrepreneurs to the country and has enabled the growth of AI startups and companies.

Overall, Canada's AI ecosystem is thriving, thanks to its collaborative research community, vibrant startup ecosystem, and government support. As the country continues to invest in AI research and innovation, we can expect to see even more exciting developments emerge from Canada in the years to come, further solidifying its position as a global leader in artificial intelligence.

Prominent AI Research Institutions in Canada

Canada is home to several prominent AI research institutions that are at the forefront of advancements in artificial intelligence. These institutions play a crucial role in shaping the future of AI research, investment, and technological advancements in the country and beyond. In this subchapter, we will highlight some of the leading AI research institutions in Canada that are making significant contributions to the field.

One of the most well-known AI research institutions in Canada is the Vector Institute, based in Toronto. The Vector Institute is dedicated to advancing AI research and fostering collaboration between academia and industry. It conducts cutting-edge research in areas such as machine learning, deep learning, and reinforcement learning, and works closely with companies to develop AI solutions for real-world applications.

Another prominent AI research institution in Canada is the Montreal Institute for Learning Algorithms (MILA), located in Montreal. MILA is known for its expertise in deep learning and neural networks, and has made significant contributions to the development of AI technologies. The institute collaborates with industry partners to translate its research into practical applications, and has helped put Canada on the map as a global hub for AI innovation.

The Alberta Machine Intelligence Institute (Amii) is another leading AI research institution in Canada, based in Edmonton. Amii focuses on machine learning and reinforcement learning, and works closely with companies to accelerate the adoption of AI technologies. The institute offers training programs and workshops to help professionals enhance their AI skills, and is actively involved in promoting AI research and innovation in Alberta and beyond.

The Canadian Institute for Advanced Research (CIFAR) is a multidisciplinary research institute that supports AI research through its AI & Society program. CIFAR brings together leading researchers from various disciplines to collaborate on AI projects that address societal challenges and opportunities. The institute's work has led to significant advancements in AI ethics, fairness, and transparency, and has helped shape the global conversation on the responsible development of AI technologies.

In addition to these institutions, Canada is home to several other AI research centers and labs that are driving innovation in the field. These institutions play a critical role in advancing AI research, investment, and technological advancements in Canada, and are helping position the country as a key player in the global AI landscape. As AI continues to transform industries and society, the work of these institutions will be instrumental in shaping the future of AI research and innovation.

Canadian AI Companies to Watch

In recent years, Canada has emerged as a hotbed for artificial intelligence (AI) innovation, with a number of companies making significant strides in the field. From healthcare to finance to transportation, Canadian AI companies are at the forefront of developing cutting-edge technologies that are shaping the future of AI. In this subchapter, we will take a closer look at some of the top Canadian AI companies to watch in the coming years.

One of the most prominent Canadian AI companies is Element AI, founded in 2016 in Montreal. Element AI is known for its work in developing AI solutions for businesses, with a focus on areas such as natural language processing, computer vision, and reinforcement learning. The company has received significant investment from both private and public sources, and its innovative approach to AI has garnered attention from around the world.

Another Canadian AI company that is making waves in the industry is Kindred, based in Toronto. Kindred specializes in developing AI-powered robots for e-commerce fulfillment centers, with a focus on improving efficiency and productivity in warehouse operations. The company's advanced AI algorithms enable its robots to perform complex tasks with precision and speed, making them a valuable asset for businesses looking to streamline their operations.

Sensely is another Canadian AI company that is worth keeping an eye on. Founded in Vancouver, Sensely is a leader in developing AI-powered virtual healthcare assistants that help patients manage their health and wellness. The company's virtual assistants use natural language processing and machine learning to provide personalized support and guidance to users, making it easier for them to access the care they need.

In addition to these companies, there are a number of other Canadian AI companies that are driving innovation and pushing the boundaries of what is possible with AI technology. From startups to established players, Canada's AI ecosystem is rich with talent and potential, making it an exciting time to be involved in the field. As AI continues to evolve and expand, Canadian companies are poised to play a key role in shaping the future of the industry.

Overall, Canadian AI companies are making a name for themselves on the global stage, with their innovative technologies and forward-thinking approach to AI. As the industry continues to grow and evolve, these companies are sure to be at the forefront of driving change and pushing the boundaries of what is possible with AI. For investors, researchers, and technologists alike, keeping an eye on Canadian AI companies is essential for staying ahead of the curve in this rapidly evolving field.

Canada's Role in Shaping the Future of AI

Canada has emerged as a key player in the field of artificial intelligence (AI), with a growing reputation for innovation and cutting-edge research. The country's role in shaping the future of AI cannot be understated, as it continues to attract top talent and investment from around the globe. Canada's commitment to advancing AI technology has positioned it as a leader in the field, alongside other tech powerhouses like the United States, China, and the United Kingdom.

One of the key factors driving Canada's success in AI is its strong academic and research institutions. Canadian universities, such as the University of Toronto and McGill University, are renowned for their AI research and have produced some of the brightest minds in the field. In addition, the Canadian government has made significant investments in AI research and development, providing funding and support for initiatives that are pushing the boundaries of what is possible with artificial intelligence.

Canada's thriving AI ecosystem has also attracted a growing number of tech companies and startups to the country. The government's supportive policies and programs, such as the Global Skills Strategy and the Strategic Innovation Fund, have made it easier for companies to establish a presence in Canada and access the talent and resources they need to succeed. As a result, Canada has become a hub for AI innovation, with companies like Element AI and DeepMind choosing to set up shop in the country.

In recent years, Canada has also taken steps to address the ethical and social implications of AI, recognizing the importance of ensuring that the technology is developed and deployed in a responsible manner. The Pan-Canadian Artificial Intelligence Strategy, launched in 2017, aims to promote the responsible use of AI and ensure that the benefits of the technology are shared equitably across society. By taking a proactive approach to AI ethics, Canada is setting an example for other countries to follow and helping to shape the future of AI in a positive and sustainable way.

In conclusion, Canada's role in shaping the future of AI is undeniable, as the country continues to make significant contributions to the field through its research, innovation, and commitment to ethical AI development. As AI research, investment, and technological advancements continue to drive progress in countries around the world, Canada stands out as a key player that is helping to shape the future of this transformative technology. With its world-class talent, supportive ecosystem, and focus on responsible AI, Canada is well-positioned to lead the way in shaping a future where artificial intelligence benefits society as a whole.

Chapter 7: France

Advancements in AI Research in France

France has been making significant strides in the field of AI research in recent years, positioning itself as a key player in the global AI landscape. The country has a long history of innovation in technology and is home to some of the world's leading AI research institutions and companies. With a strong focus on interdisciplinary collaboration and cutting-edge research, France has been at the forefront of developing AI solutions that have the potential to revolutionize industries and improve the quality of life for people around the world.

One of the key advancements in AI research in France is the development of sophisticated algorithms for machine learning and deep learning. French researchers have been at the forefront of developing new techniques and models that have significantly improved the performance of AI systems in a wide range of applications, from natural language processing to computer vision. These advancements have paved the way for the development of AI-powered solutions that are more accurate, efficient, and scalable than ever before, opening up new possibilities for AI-driven innovation in various industries.

Another area where France has made significant progress in AI research is in the field of robotics and autonomous systems. French researchers have been working on developing advanced robotic systems that can perform complex tasks autonomously, such as navigating through challenging environments, manipulating objects with precision, and interacting with humans in a natural and intuitive way. These advancements have the potential to revolutionize industries such as manufacturing, healthcare, and transportation, where robots can play a key role in increasing efficiency, productivity, and safety.

In addition to advancements in AI algorithms and robotics, France has also been investing heavily in building a robust ecosystem for AI research and innovation. The country has established AI research centers, incubators, and accelerators that bring together researchers, startups, and industry partners to collaborate on cutting-edge AI projects. These initiatives have helped foster a culture of innovation and entrepreneurship in France, attracting top talent from around the world and positioning the country as a hub for AI research and investment.

Overall, France's advancements in AI research are shaping the future of AI technology and driving innovation in a wide range of industries. With a strong emphasis on collaboration, interdisciplinary research, and investment in talent and infrastructure, France is well-positioned to continue leading the way in AI research and development in the years to come, contributing to the global advancement of AI technology and its impact on society.

French AI Companies Leading the Way

In the competitive landscape of AI research and development, French companies are quickly emerging as leaders in the field. With a strong emphasis on innovation and collaboration, these companies are making significant strides in pushing the boundaries of artificial intelligence technology. From machine learning algorithms to natural language processing, French AI companies are at the forefront of cutting-edge research and development.

One such company leading the way in AI innovation is Criteo, a global technology company specializing in performance marketing. Leveraging AI and machine learning algorithms, Criteo has revolutionized the way online advertising is targeted and personalized for individual users.

Through its advanced algorithms, Criteo is able to deliver highly relevant and personalized ads to consumers, resulting in higher conversion rates and increased revenue for its clients.

Another standout French AI company is Dataiku, a leading provider of data science and machine learning platforms. With its user-friendly interface and powerful tools, Dataiku enables organizations to easily build and deploy AI models for a wide range of applications, from predictive analytics to image recognition. By democratizing AI technology, Dataiku is empowering companies of all sizes to harness the power of artificial intelligence for improved decision-making and business outcomes.

French AI companies are also making waves in the healthcare industry, with companies like Owkin leading the charge in using artificial intelligence to revolutionize medical research and treatment. By applying machine learning algorithms to vast amounts of medical data, Owkin is able to identify patterns and insights that can lead to more personalized and effective treatments for patients. Through its innovative approach to AI-driven healthcare, Owkin is paving the way for a more efficient and patient-centric healthcare system.

Overall, French AI companies are playing a crucial role in shaping the future of artificial intelligence technology. With their focus on innovation, collaboration, and cutting-edge research, these companies are driving advancements in AI technology that have the potential to transform industries and improve the lives of people around the world. As the global AI landscape continues to evolve, French companies will undoubtedly remain at the forefront of AI research, investment, and technological advancements.

Government Investment in AI in France

France has been making significant strides in the field of artificial intelligence (AI) in recent years, thanks in part to the government's investment in the technology. The French government has recognized the importance of AI in driving innovation and economic growth, and has made it a priority to support research and development in this area. As a result, France has emerged as a leading player in the global AI landscape, attracting top talent and investment from around the world.

One of the key initiatives driving AI investment in France is the national AI strategy launched by President Emmanuel Macron in 2018. The strategy aims to position France as a global leader in AI by investing in research, talent development, and infrastructure. The government has committed to investing €1.5 billion in AI by 2022, with a focus on key areas such as healthcare, transportation, and cybersecurity. These investments have already begun to bear fruit, with French companies and research institutions making significant advancements in AI technologies.

In addition to financial support, the French government has also taken steps to foster collaboration between academia, industry, and government in the AI space. For example, the government has established AI research institutes and innovation hubs to facilitate knowledge sharing and collaboration. These initiatives have helped to create a vibrant ecosystem for AI research and development in France, attracting top researchers and entrepreneurs from around the world.

Furthermore, the French government has been proactive in addressing ethical and regulatory concerns related to AI. In 2019, France became the first country in Europe to adopt a national AI strategy that includes guidelines for the ethical development and deployment of AI technologies. This commitment to responsible AI innovation has helped to build trust among consumers and businesses, further driving investment in the sector.

Overall, France's government investment in AI has positioned the country as a key player in the global AI landscape. By supporting research, fostering collaboration, and addressing ethical concerns, France has created a conducive environment for AI innovation and investment. As the technology continues to evolve, France is well positioned to lead the way in shaping the future of AI.

Collaboration with European Partners in AI

In recent years, the field of artificial intelligence (AI) has seen significant growth and development around the globe. As countries such as the United States, China, United Kingdom, Israel, Canada, France, India, Japan, Germany, and Singapore continue to invest heavily in AI research, it has become increasingly important for these nations to collaborate with their European counterparts in order to advance the field. This subchapter will explore the benefits of collaboration with European partners in AI and highlight some key initiatives that are currently underway.

One of the main advantages of collaborating with European partners in AI is the opportunity to leverage the diverse expertise and resources that are available in the region. European countries such as Germany, France, and the United Kingdom have long been at the forefront of AI research and development, and they have established strong networks of academic institutions, research centers, and industry partners that can provide valuable insights and support for collaborative projects. By working together with European partners, countries like the United States, China, and Japan can access cutting-edge technologies and innovative solutions that can help them stay competitive in the global AI market.

Another benefit of collaborating with European partners in AI is the opportunity to access a larger pool of talent and expertise. European countries have a strong tradition of investing in education and research, and they have produced a large number of highly skilled AI professionals who are leading the way in fields such as machine learning, natural language processing, and computer vision. By partnering with European institutions and companies, countries like Israel, Canada, and Singapore can tap into this talent pool and benefit from the fresh ideas and perspectives that European researchers bring to the table.

In addition to accessing expertise and talent, collaborating with European partners in AI can also help countries to address common challenges and opportunities in the field. For example, many European countries are facing similar issues around data privacy, ethics, and regulation in AI, and by working together, they can develop shared frameworks and standards that can help to address these issues in a consistent and effective manner. By collaborating with European partners, countries like India, France, and the United Kingdom can also explore new markets and business opportunities that can help them to expand their AI capabilities and drive economic growth.

Overall, collaboration with European partners in AI offers a wide range of benefits for countries that are looking to advance their research, investment, and technological advancements in the field. By working together with European institutions, companies, and researchers, countries like the United States, China, and Germany can access valuable expertise, talent, and resources, and develop innovative solutions that can help them to stay at the forefront of the global AI market. As the field of AI continues to evolve and expand, collaboration with European partners will be essential for countries that are looking to drive innovation and make a meaningful impact in the field.

Chapter 8: India

Rise of AI in India

The Rise of AI in India

India, known for its rich history and diverse culture, is quickly emerging as a major player in the field of artificial intelligence. With a growing economy and a large pool of talented engineers and researchers, India is poised to become a global leader in AI research, investment, and technological advancements. In recent years, the Indian government has made significant investments in AI research and development, leading to the establishment of several world-class research institutions and labs dedicated to advancing the field.

One of the key drivers of the rise of AI in India is the country's strong focus on education and innovation. Indian universities and research institutions are producing a steady stream of highly skilled graduates in computer science, engineering, and related fields, many of whom are now leading groundbreaking research in AI. In addition, India is home to a vibrant startup ecosystem, with a growing number of AI companies attracting significant investment from both domestic and international sources.

The Indian government has also recognized the importance of AI in driving economic growth and improving the quality of life for its citizens. In 2018, India launched the National AI Strategy, a comprehensive plan to promote the development and adoption of AI technologies across various sectors, including healthcare, agriculture, and transportation. The strategy aims to position India as a global hub for AI research and innovation, and to leverage AI to address some of the country's most pressing challenges.

Despite these advancements, India still faces several challenges in realizing its full potential in the field of AI. Limited access to high-quality data, a shortage of AI talent, and a lack of investment in research infrastructure are some of the key obstacles that the country must overcome. However, with the right support and investments, India has the potential to become a major player in the global AI landscape, driving innovation and creating new opportunities for growth and development.

As India continues to make strides in AI research, investment, and technological advancements, it is clear that the country's unique strengths and capabilities position it as a key player in shaping the future of AI on the global stage. With a growing ecosystem of talent, resources, and innovation, India is poised to play a significant role in driving the next wave of AI-powered technologies and solutions that will impact industries and societies around the world.

Indian Tech Giants Investing in AI

In recent years, Indian tech giants have been making significant investments in artificial intelligence (AI) technology. Companies like Tata Consultancy Services, Infosys, and Wipro are leading the charge in developing AI solutions that cater to a wide range of industries, from healthcare to finance to manufacturing. These companies are leveraging India's strong talent pool in engineering and computer science to create cutting-edge AI algorithms that are changing the way businesses operate.

One of the key areas where Indian tech giants are investing in AI is in the healthcare sector. With the rise of telemedicine and remote patient monitoring, there is a growing need for AI-powered solutions that can analyze vast amounts of data and provide insights to healthcare professionals. Companies like Tata Consultancy Services are developing AI algorithms that can predict patient outcomes, recommend personalized treatment plans, and identify potential health risks before they escalate.

In addition to healthcare, Indian tech giants are also focusing on AI solutions for the financial services industry. With the rise of digital banking and fintech startups, there is a growing demand for AI-powered tools that can automate processes, detect fraud, and improve customer service. Companies like Infosys are developing AI chatbots that can assist customers with their banking needs, while Wipro is working on AI algorithms that can analyze market trends and make investment recommendations.

Another area where Indian tech giants are making strides in AI is in the manufacturing sector. With the rise of Industry 4.0 and smart factories, there is a growing need for AI-powered solutions that can optimize production processes, reduce downtime, and improve quality control. Companies like Tata Consultancy Services are developing AI algorithms that can analyze sensor data from machines, predict maintenance issues before they occur, and optimize production schedules to meet customer demand.

Overall, Indian tech giants are playing a crucial role in the development and adoption of AI technology in various industries. By leveraging India's strong talent pool and expertise in engineering and computer science, these companies are creating innovative AI solutions that are driving digital transformation and revolutionizing the way businesses operate. As AI continues to evolve and become more integrated into everyday life, Indian tech giants will undoubtedly play a key role in shaping the future of AI on a global scale.

Government Initiatives to Boost AI Adoption

In recent years, governments around the world have recognized the potential of artificial intelligence (AI) to revolutionize industries and drive economic growth. As a result, many countries have launched initiatives to boost AI adoption and development within their borders. These initiatives range from funding for AI research and development to the creation of regulatory frameworks to support the responsible use of AI technologies.

One of the most notable government initiatives to boost AI adoption is the United States' AI Initiative, launched in 2019. This initiative aims to accelerate AI research and development, promote AI ethics and safety, and ensure the United States remains a global leader in AI technologies. Through partnerships with industry, academia, and other stakeholders, the U.S. government is working to drive innovation and create new opportunities for AI adoption in sectors such as healthcare, transportation, and defense.

Similarly, China has made significant investments in AI research and development through its "New Generation Artificial Intelligence Development Plan." This initiative aims to make China the world leader in AI technologies by 2030 and has already resulted in the creation of AI research centers, funding for AI startups, and the development of AI-powered infrastructure projects. By investing heavily in AI, China hopes to drive economic growth and improve the quality of life for its citizens.

In the United Kingdom, the government has launched the AI Sector Deal to support the growth of the AI industry and boost AI adoption across various sectors. This initiative includes funding for AI research and development, support for AI startups, and the creation of AI-focused educational programs. By investing in AI, the UK government aims to create new opportunities for economic growth and establish the UK as a global hub for AI innovation.

Other countries, such as Israel, Canada, France, India, Japan, Germany, and Singapore, have also launched government initiatives to boost AI adoption and development. These initiatives include funding for AI research and development, the creation of regulatory frameworks to support AI adoption, and partnerships with industry stakeholders to drive innovation. By supporting AI adoption, these countries hope to drive economic growth, create new opportunities for innovation, and improve the quality of life for their citizens.

Challenges and Opportunities in Indian AI Industry

The Indian AI industry is currently facing a number of challenges, but also presents numerous opportunities for growth and innovation. One of the main challenges facing the industry is the lack of skilled AI professionals. While India is home to a large pool of talented engineers and developers, there is a shortage of individuals with specialized knowledge in artificial intelligence. This has led to fierce competition for top talent, driving up salaries and making it difficult for smaller companies to attract and retain skilled employees.

Another challenge facing the Indian AI industry is the lack of infrastructure and resources. While major cities like Bangalore and Hyderabad have established themselves as hubs for tech innovation, many parts of the country still lack access to high-speed internet and other essential resources. This can make it difficult for companies to develop and deploy AI solutions, limiting their ability to compete on a global scale.

Despite these challenges, the Indian AI industry also presents a number of opportunities for growth and innovation. One of the key advantages of the Indian market is its large and diverse population. This provides a wealth of data that can be used to train AI models and develop innovative solutions for a wide range of industries. In addition, the country's rapidly growing economy and increasing investment in technology make it an attractive destination for AI research, investment, and technological advancements.

Furthermore, India's strong focus on education and research in the STEM fields has produced a new generation of talented AI professionals. Many universities and research institutions in the country are actively engaged in cutting-edge research in artificial intelligence, creating a strong foundation for future growth in the industry. This, combined with the government's recent initiatives to promote AI development, such as the National AI Portal and the National AI Strategy, bode well for the future of the Indian AI industry.

In conclusion, while the Indian AI industry faces challenges such as a shortage of skilled professionals and limited infrastructure, it also presents numerous opportunities for growth and innovation. With its large and diverse population, strong focus on education and research, and increasing investment in technology, India is well-positioned to become a major player in the global AI market. By addressing these challenges and capitalizing on its strengths, the Indian AI industry has the potential to drive significant advancements in AI research, investment, and technological advancements in the years to come.

Chapter 9: Japan

AI Innovation in Japan

In recent years, Japan has emerged as a powerhouse in the field of artificial intelligence (AI) innovation. With a long history of technological advancements and a strong focus on research and development, Japan has become a key player in the global AI landscape. From robotics to machine learning, Japanese companies and research institutions are at the forefront of cutting-edge AI technologies.

One of the key areas of AI innovation in Japan is robotics. Japanese companies like SoftBank Robotics and Sony have been leading the way in developing humanoid robots that can interact with humans in a natural and intuitive way. These robots are being used in a variety of industries, from healthcare to entertainment, and are helping to revolutionize the way we interact with technology.

In addition to robotics, Japan is also making significant strides in the field of machine learning. Japanese researchers are working on developing advanced algorithms and models that can analyze and interpret vast amounts of data with unprecedented accuracy and speed. These advancements are being applied in sectors such as finance, healthcare, and transportation, where AI-powered systems are helping to optimize processes and improve decision-making.

Furthermore, Japan's government has been actively supporting AI research and development through initiatives like the Japan AI Strategy, which aims to position Japan as a global leader in AI by 2030. The strategy includes investments in AI education, infrastructure, and collaboration between industry and academia, creating a fertile ground for innovation and growth in the AI sector.

Overall, Japan's AI innovation is a testament to the country's commitment to staying at the forefront of technological advancements. With its strong research capabilities, innovative companies, and supportive government policies, Japan is well-positioned to continue driving progress in the field of artificial intelligence and shaping the future of AI on a global scale.

Japanese Companies at the Forefront of AI

Japan is well-known for its technological advancements, and the field of artificial intelligence is no exception. In recent years, Japanese companies have been making significant strides in the development of AI technologies, positioning themselves at the forefront of innovation in this rapidly growing industry.

One of the key players in the Japanese AI landscape is SoftBank Robotics, a subsidiary of SoftBank Group. The company is known for its humanoid robot Pepper, which has gained popularity around the world for its ability to interact with humans in a natural and intuitive way. SoftBank Robotics is also working on developing AI-powered solutions for a wide range of industries, from healthcare to retail.

Another notable Japanese company in the AI space is Preferred Networks, a Tokyo-based startup that specializes in deep learning technologies. The company has been collaborating with major Japanese corporations to develop AI solutions for autonomous driving, healthcare, and other industries. Preferred Networks' cutting-edge research in AI has garnered the attention of investors and researchers alike, solidifying its position as a leader in the field.

In addition to startups and established companies, Japanese universities and research institutions are also contributing to the advancement of AI technology. The University of Tokyo, for example, has a strong research program in artificial intelligence, with a focus on machine learning, computer vision, and natural language processing. Researchers at the university are collaborating with industry partners to develop AI solutions that address real-world challenges.

Overall, the Japanese AI ecosystem is vibrant and diverse, with companies of all sizes and research institutions working together to push the boundaries of what is possible with artificial intelligence. As the global demand for AI technologies continues to grow, Japanese companies are well-positioned to play a key role in shaping the future of this rapidly evolving industry. With their innovative spirit and commitment to excellence, Japanese companies are poised to make a lasting impact on the world of artificial intelligence.

Japan's AI Strategy for Economic Growth

Japan has long been a pioneer in technological advancements, leading the world in various industries such as automotive, electronics, and robotics. In recent years, Japan has also set its sights on becoming a global leader in artificial intelligence (AI) technology. The country's AI strategy for economic growth is a comprehensive plan that encompasses various initiatives aimed at fostering innovation, research, and development in the field of AI.

One of the key elements of Japan's AI strategy is its focus on investing in research and development. The Japanese government has allocated significant funds to support AI research projects in both the public and private sectors. This investment has led to the establishment of numerous AI research centers and laboratories across the country, where scientists and researchers are working on cutting-edge AI technologies.

Another important aspect of Japan's AI strategy is its emphasis on collaboration and partnerships. The government has been actively promoting collaboration between academia, industry, and government agencies to facilitate knowledge sharing and technology transfer. This collaborative approach has helped accelerate the development and adoption of AI technologies in various sectors, including healthcare, finance, manufacturing, and transportation.

Furthermore, Japan is also focusing on developing a skilled workforce capable of driving innovation and growth in the AI sector. The country has been investing in AI education and training programs to equip its workforce with the necessary skills and expertise to work in the field of AI. In addition, Japan is also attracting top AI talent from around the world through initiatives such as visa programs and research grants.

Overall, Japan's AI strategy for economic growth is a holistic approach that encompasses investment, collaboration, and talent development. By leveraging its strengths in technology and innovation, Japan is well-positioned to become a global leader in AI technology and drive economic growth in the coming years. With its unwavering commitment to AI research, investment, and technological advancements, Japan is poised to shape the future of AI on a global scale.

Future Outlook for AI in Japan

As one of the leading technological hubs in the world, Japan has been at the forefront of AI research, investment, and technological advancements. The country has a long history of innovation in robotics and automation, making it a natural fit for the development of AI technologies. With a strong emphasis on precision and efficiency, Japan has the potential to become a major player in the global AI market.

One of the key areas of focus for AI development in Japan is the integration of AI into everyday life. From self-driving cars to smart homes, Japanese companies are exploring ways to make AI more accessible and user-friendly. By incorporating AI into various aspects of daily life, Japan aims to improve efficiency, convenience, and overall quality of life for its citizens.

Another important trend in the future outlook for AI in Japan is the collaboration between government, industry, and academia. The Japanese government has been actively promoting AI research and development through initiatives such as the AI R&D Strategy Council. By fostering partnerships between researchers, businesses, and government agencies, Japan hopes to accelerate the pace of AI innovation and ensure that the country remains competitive in the global market.

In addition to domestic initiatives, Japan is also looking to expand its influence in the global AI market. With a strong track record in robotics and automation, Japanese companies are well-positioned to compete on the international stage. By leveraging its technological expertise and strong industrial base, Japan can establish itself as a key player in the development and deployment of AI technologies around the world.

Overall, the future outlook for AI in Japan is bright. With a strong emphasis on innovation, collaboration, and international competitiveness, Japan is well-positioned to lead the way in the development of AI technologies. By harnessing its strengths in robotics, automation, and precision engineering, Japan can continue to push the boundaries of what is possible with AI and shape the future of technology for years to come.

Chapter 10: Germany

AI Research and Development in Germany

Germany has long been at the forefront of AI research and development, with a strong focus on innovation and collaboration between industry and academia. The country is home to a number of world-renowned research institutions, such as the Max Planck Institute for Intelligent Systems and the German Research Center for Artificial Intelligence (DFKI), which are leading the way in cutting-edge AI research.

One of the key areas of focus in AI research and development in Germany is machine learning, particularly in the fields of deep learning and neural networks. German researchers have made significant contributions to the advancement of these technologies, with a number of breakthroughs in areas such as natural language processing, computer vision, and reinforcement learning.

In addition to its academic research institutions, Germany is also home to a thriving AI startup ecosystem, with companies such as Merantix and Twenty Billion Neurons gaining international recognition for their work in AI. The country's strong industrial base, particularly in sectors such as automotive and manufacturing, has also provided fertile ground for the development and application of AI technologies.

Germany's commitment to AI research and development is further evidenced by the government's recent announcement of a €3 billion investment in AI by 2025. This funding will support initiatives to promote AI innovation and adoption across various sectors, with a particular focus on ensuring that Germany remains competitive in the global AI landscape.

Overall, Germany's strong tradition of scientific excellence, coupled with its thriving startup ecosystem and government support, position the country as a key player in the future of AI research and development. With a focus on collaboration, innovation, and investment, Germany is poised to continue driving advancements in AI technologies that will benefit not only the country itself, but the global AI community as a whole.

German Companies Driving AI Innovation

In recent years, Germany has emerged as a key player in driving AI innovation on a global scale. German companies have been at the forefront of developing cutting-edge technologies and solutions that are shaping the future of AI. With a strong emphasis on research and development, Germany has become a hub for AI research, investment, and technological advancements.

One of the key drivers of AI innovation in Germany is the country's strong focus on collaboration between industry and academia. German companies work closely with leading research institutions and universities to develop innovative AI solutions that address real-world challenges. This collaborative approach has led to the creation of groundbreaking technologies in areas such as autonomous vehicles, healthcare, and manufacturing.

German companies are also known for their commitment to ethical AI development. With a focus on transparency, fairness, and accountability, German companies are leading the way in ensuring that AI technologies are developed and deployed in a responsible manner. This commitment to ethical AI has helped Germany establish itself as a trusted partner in the global AI community.

Furthermore, Germany's strong regulatory environment and commitment to data privacy have also played a key role in driving AI innovation in the country. With strict regulations in place to protect consumer data and ensure transparency in AI development, German companies have been able to build trust with consumers and investors alike. This regulatory framework has helped foster a culture of innovation and responsible AI development in Germany.

Overall, German companies are making significant contributions to the field of AI and are driving innovation in key industries around the world. With a focus on collaboration, ethics, and regulatory compliance, Germany is well-positioned to continue leading the way in AI research, investment, and technological advancements on a global scale.

Collaboration between Industry and Academia in AI

In the rapidly evolving field of artificial intelligence (AI), collaboration between industry and academia is crucial for advancing research, driving innovation, and accelerating technological advancements. This subchapter explores the various ways in which partnerships between industry and academia in the United States, China, United Kingdom, Israel, Canada, France, India, Japan, Germany, and Singapore are shaping the future of AI.

In the United States, renowned institutions such as Stanford University, MIT, and Carnegie Mellon University have established strong ties with leading tech companies like Google, Facebook, and Amazon. These partnerships have led to groundbreaking research in areas such as machine learning, natural language processing, and computer vision. By working together, academia and industry are able to leverage their respective strengths and resources to address complex challenges in AI.

In China, companies like Baidu, Alibaba, and Tencent have formed collaborative relationships with top universities such as Tsinghua University and Peking University. These partnerships have enabled Chinese researchers to make significant advancements in AI, particularly in the areas of deep learning and big data analytics. The Chinese government has also played a key role in fostering collaboration between industry and academia through initiatives like the National AI Development Plan.

In the United Kingdom, institutions like the University of Cambridge, Imperial College London, and Oxford University have established partnerships with companies like DeepMind and OpenAI. These collaborations have led to breakthroughs in AI research, particularly in the fields of reinforcement learning and robotics. The UK government has also been actively supporting collaborations between industry and academia through funding programs and policy initiatives.

In Israel, companies like Mobileye, Waze, and Intel have collaborated with academic institutions such as the Technion-Israel Institute of Technology and the Hebrew University of Jerusalem. These partnerships have driven innovation in AI applications for autonomous vehicles, cybersecurity, and healthcare. The Israeli government has also been instrumental in facilitating collaboration between industry and academia through programs like the Israel Innovation Authority.

In Canada, institutions like the University of Toronto, McGill University, and the University of British Columbia have forged partnerships with companies like Element AI and Deep Genomics. These collaborations have led to significant advancements in AI research, particularly in the areas of reinforcement learning, healthcare, and natural language processing. The Canadian government has also been supportive of collaborations between industry and academia through initiatives like the Pan-Canadian Artificial Intelligence Strategy.

Germany's Competitive Advantage in AI

Germany has emerged as a key player in the field of artificial intelligence (AI), boasting a competitive advantage that sets it apart from other global competitors. One of the main reasons for Germany's success in AI is its strong emphasis on research and development. The country is home to several world-class research institutions and universities that are at the forefront of AI innovation. This commitment to research has allowed Germany to produce cutting-edge technologies and solutions that are in high demand worldwide.

Furthermore, Germany's strong industrial base has also contributed to its competitive advantage in AI. The country is known for its advanced manufacturing sector, which has embraced AI technologies to improve efficiency, productivity, and competitiveness. This integration of AI into traditional industries has given Germany a unique edge in the global market, allowing it to stay ahead of the curve and drive innovation in various sectors.

In addition, Germany's robust investment in AI has played a crucial role in its competitive advantage. The government has allocated significant funding towards AI research and development, as well as initiatives to support AI startups and businesses. This proactive approach to investment has created a fertile ground for AI innovation to thrive, attracting top talent and fostering a vibrant ecosystem of AI companies and entrepreneurs.

Moreover, Germany's strong focus on ethics and data privacy has also set it apart in the field of AI. The country has strict regulations in place to protect user data and ensure the responsible use of AI technologies. This commitment to ethical AI practices has not only earned Germany a reputation as a trustworthy partner in the global AI landscape but has also positioned it as a leader in shaping the future of AI governance and policy.

Overall, Germany's competitive advantage in AI can be attributed to its strong research and development capabilities, advanced industrial base, strategic investment in AI, and commitment to ethics and data privacy. As the country continues to lead the way in AI innovation, it is poised to play a pivotal role in shaping the future of AI on a global scale.

Chapter 11: Singapore

Singapore's AI Landscape

Singapore has emerged as a key player in the global AI landscape, with a rapidly growing ecosystem that is attracting attention from around the world. The city-state has positioned itself as a hub for AI research, investment, and technological advancements, thanks to its strategic location, strong government support, and world-class talent pool.

In recent years, Singapore has made significant investments in AI research and development, with the government launching initiatives such as the AI Singapore program to drive innovation in the sector. This has led to the establishment of cutting-edge research centers and collaborations with leading universities and tech companies, further cementing Singapore's reputation as a hotbed for AI innovation.

The investment landscape in Singapore is also thriving, with a number of venture capital firms and investors pouring funds into AI startups and companies. The city-state's pro-business environment, strong intellectual property protection laws, and access to global markets make it an attractive destination for AI investments, leading to a surge in funding rounds and acquisitions in the sector.

On the technological front, Singapore is at the forefront of AI adoption, with companies across industries harnessing the power of AI to drive efficiencies, enhance customer experiences, and unlock new revenue streams. From healthcare and finance to manufacturing and logistics, Singapore is leveraging AI technologies such as machine learning, natural language processing, and computer vision to stay ahead of the curve.

Overall, Singapore's AI landscape is vibrant and dynamic, offering a wealth of opportunities for AI research, investment, and technological advancements. With its strategic focus on AI innovation, strong government support, and thriving ecosystem, Singapore is well-positioned to shape the future of AI on a global scale, making it a key player to watch in the AI arena.

Key Players in Singapore's AI Industry

Singapore has quickly become a hub for AI research, investment, and technological advancements, attracting key players in the industry from around the globe. The city-state's strategic location, world-class infrastructure, and supportive government policies have made it an attractive destination for companies looking to establish a presence in the region. In this subchapter, we will explore some of the key players in Singapore's AI industry and the contributions they are making to the field.

One of the most prominent players in Singapore's AI industry is SenseTime, a Chinese company that specializes in facial recognition technology. SenseTime has established a strong presence in Singapore, working closely with government agencies and private companies to develop cutting-edge AI solutions. The company's advanced algorithms have been used in a variety of applications, from security surveillance to healthcare diagnostics, making it a key player in the development of AI technology in the region.

Another key player in Singapore's AI industry is Grab, a Southeast Asian technology company that offers a wide range of services, including ride-hailing, food delivery, and digital payments. Grab has made significant investments in AI technology, using machine learning algorithms to optimize its services and improve the user experience. The company's AI initiatives have helped it stay ahead of the competition and establish itself as a leader in the region's tech ecosystem.

Singapore-based AI startup, Taiger, is also making waves in the industry with its innovative natural language processing technology. The company's AI-powered solutions are used by businesses in various sectors, including finance, healthcare, and legal services, to automate processes and improve efficiency. Taiger's cutting-edge technology has garnered international recognition, positioning the company as a key player in Singapore's AI landscape.

Additionally, NCS, a leading IT services provider in Singapore, has been actively involved in the development and deployment of AI solutions across various industries. The company's AI expertise spans areas such as data analytics, robotic process automation, and machine learning, enabling businesses to harness the power of AI to drive growth and innovation. NCS's contributions to the advancement of AI technology in Singapore have solidified its position as a key player in the industry.

Overall, Singapore's AI industry is thriving, thanks to the contributions of key players like SenseTime, Grab, Taiger, and NCS. These companies are at the forefront of innovation, driving growth and technological advancements in the region. As Singapore continues to position itself as a global AI hub, the collaboration and expertise of these key players will be instrumental in shaping the future of AI research, investment, and technological advancements in the city-state and beyond.

Government Support for AI in Singapore

Singapore has been at the forefront of embracing artificial intelligence (AI) technology, recognizing its potential to drive economic growth and improve the lives of its citizens. The government of Singapore has shown strong support for AI through various initiatives and policies aimed at fostering innovation and research in this field. One of the key ways in which the Singaporean government supports AI is through funding and grants for AI research projects. This financial support has helped to attract top AI talent to Singapore and has enabled the country to establish itself as a hub for AI innovation in the region.

In addition to providing financial support, the Singaporean government has also taken steps to create a conducive environment for AI development. This includes the establishment of AI-focused research centers and institutes, such as the AI Singapore program, which aims to promote AI research and development in the country. The government has also worked to streamline regulations and policies related to AI, to ensure that businesses and researchers have the necessary support and guidance to work on AI projects.

Furthermore, the Singaporean government has made significant investments in AI infrastructure, such as developing data centers and networks to support the processing and storage of large amounts of data required for AI applications. This investment in infrastructure has helped to position Singapore as a leading player in the AI industry, attracting companies and researchers from around the world to collaborate and innovate in the country.

The government's support for AI in Singapore has also extended to the education sector, with initiatives aimed at equipping students with the skills and knowledge needed to work in the AI industry. This includes the introduction of AI courses and programs in schools and universities, as well as partnerships with industry players to provide students with hands-on experience in AI projects. By investing in education and training, the Singaporean government is ensuring that the country has a steady supply of skilled AI professionals to drive innovation and growth in this field.

Overall, the government's support for AI in Singapore has been instrumental in positioning the country as a global leader in AI research, investment, and technological advancements. By providing funding, creating a conducive environment for development, investing in infrastructure, and promoting education and training, the Singaporean government is paving the way for a future powered by AI innovation and excellence.

Singapore's Position as an AI Hub in Asia

Singapore has quickly emerged as a leading hub for artificial intelligence (AI) in Asia, attracting top talent, companies, and investments from around the world. With its strategic location, pro-business environment, and strong government support for innovation, Singapore has positioned itself as a key player in the global AI landscape. The city-state has set ambitious goals to become a Smart Nation, leveraging AI technologies to drive economic growth, improve quality of life, and enhance government services.

Singapore's success as an AI hub can be attributed to its strong focus on research and development in AI. The country boasts world-class research institutions such as the National University of Singapore (NUS) and the Agency for Science, Technology and Research (A*STAR), which are at the forefront of AI innovation. These institutions collaborate with industry partners to develop cutting-edge AI solutions in areas such as healthcare, finance, transportation, and cybersecurity. Singapore's vibrant AI ecosystem also includes startups, accelerators, and venture capital firms that are driving innovation and entrepreneurship in the AI space.

In addition to its research capabilities, Singapore offers a conducive environment for AI investments and technological advancements. The country's robust intellectual property protection, strong legal framework, and business-friendly policies make it an attractive destination for AI companies looking to establish a presence in Asia. Singapore's government has also launched initiatives such as the AI Singapore program, which aims to accelerate AI adoption in key sectors and build a pipeline of AI talent. These efforts have helped Singapore attract top AI talent from around the world and foster a culture of innovation and collaboration in the AI community.

Singapore's strategic location in Asia further enhances its position as an AI hub, serving as a gateway to the fast-growing markets in the region. The city-state's advanced infrastructure, world-class connectivity, and multicultural workforce make it an ideal location for AI companies to expand their operations and tap into the diverse opportunities in Asia. Singapore's government has also established partnerships with other AI hubs in the region, such as China and India, to promote collaboration and knowledge exchange in AI research, investment, and technological advancements.

Looking ahead, Singapore is well-positioned to continue its growth as a leading AI hub in Asia, leveraging its strengths in research, innovation, and collaboration to drive technological advancements and economic development. As AI continues to transform industries and societies around the world, Singapore is poised to play a key role in shaping the future of AI and driving innovation in the region. With its strategic vision, strong ecosystem, and government support, Singapore is set to remain at the forefront of AI research, investment, and technological advancements in Asia and beyond.

Chapter 12: Conclusion

Key Takeaways from Global AI Trends and Insights

In this subchapter, we will delve into the key takeaways from global AI trends and insights, focusing on the advancements in AI research, investment, and technological developments in countries such as the United States, China, United Kingdom, Israel, Canada, France, India, Japan, Germany, and Singapore. These nations are at the forefront of AI innovation, with each bringing unique perspectives and contributions to the field.

One of the key takeaways from our analysis is the significant investment being made in AI research and development in the United States. With Silicon Valley leading the charge, American companies are pouring resources into AI technologies, driving advancements in machine learning, natural language processing, and computer vision. The U.S. remains a powerhouse in AI research, attracting top talent and fostering a culture of innovation.

China, on the other hand, is rapidly emerging as a global AI leader, with the government investing heavily in AI technologies as part of its strategic plan for economic growth. Chinese companies are leveraging AI to drive advancements in industries such as healthcare, finance, and transportation, positioning the country as a key player in the global AI landscape. The United States and China are engaged in a fierce competition for AI dominance, with both nations vying for supremacy in this critical technology sector.

The United Kingdom, Israel, Canada, France, India, Japan, Germany, and Singapore are also making significant strides in AI research and development, each with its own unique strengths and areas of expertise. From cutting-edge research in deep learning to innovative applications in robotics and autonomous systems, these countries are driving advancements in AI that have far-reaching implications for industries and societies worldwide. Collaboration and knowledge-sharing between these nations will be critical in advancing the field of AI and addressing complex challenges on a global scale.

As we look to the future of AI, it is clear that collaboration and cooperation between countries will be essential in driving innovation and ensuring the responsible development and deployment of AI technologies. By learning from the successes and challenges of nations around the globe, we can work together to harness the transformative power of AI for the benefit of all. The insights and trends highlighted in this subchapter provide a valuable roadmap for AI researchers, investors, and technological advancements in the United States, China, United Kingdom, Israel, Canada, France, India, Japan, Germany, and Singapore as they navigate the complexities of the AI landscape and shape the future of this rapidly evolving field.

Implications for the Future of AI Research, Investment, and Technological Advancements

As we look towards the future of AI research, investment, and technological advancements, it is clear that the global landscape is rapidly evolving. Countries such as the United States, China, United Kingdom, Israel, Canada, France, India, Japan, Germany, and Singapore are at the forefront of AI innovation, each bringing their own unique strengths and capabilities to the table.

One of the key implications for the future of AI research is the increasing collaboration and competition among these countries. While cooperation is essential for advancing AI technologies, competition also drives innovation and pushes boundaries. As such, we can expect to see a growing number of partnerships and strategic alliances forming between these nations in the coming years, as they seek to leverage each other's expertise and resources for mutual benefit.

In terms of investment, the future of AI looks bright as well. With governments and private sector organizations pouring billions of dollars into AI research and development, we can expect to see a surge in breakthrough technologies and applications in the near future. This investment will not only drive economic growth and job creation, but also pave the way for new opportunities and challenges in the AI space.

Technological advancements in AI are also set to revolutionize industries across the globe. From healthcare and finance to transportation and manufacturing, AI has the potential to transform how we live, work, and interact with the world around us. As AI technologies become more sophisticated and widespread, we can expect to see a wave of new products and services that will enhance our daily lives and drive productivity and efficiency in ways we never thought possible.

In conclusion, the future of AI research, investment, and technological advancements holds great promise for countries around the world. By capitalizing on their strengths and collaborating with one another, these nations can drive innovation, create new opportunities, and shape the future of AI in a way that benefits society as a whole. With the right strategies and investments in place, the possibilities for AI are truly limitless, and the future is looking brighter than ever for the global AI community.

Recommendations for Stakeholders in the AI Ecosystem

In order to foster a thriving AI ecosystem, it is essential for stakeholders in the field to collaborate and share insights across borders. This will not only help in accelerating the pace of innovation but also contribute to the overall growth and development of the industry. Therefore, it is recommended that stakeholders in AI research, investment, and technological advancements in countries such as the United States, China, United Kingdom, Israel, Canada, France, India, Japan, Germany, and Singapore come together to exchange ideas and best practices.

One recommendation for stakeholders in the AI ecosystem is to invest in education and training programs that focus on developing the necessary skills for the future workforce. This will not only help in bridging the talent gap but also ensure that there is a continuous supply of skilled professionals in the field. Additionally, investing in research and development initiatives will help in pushing the boundaries of AI technology and driving innovation forward.

Another recommendation is for stakeholders to prioritize ethics and responsible AI practices in their work. This includes promoting transparency, accountability, and fairness in AI algorithms and decision-making processes. By adhering to ethical guidelines and standards, stakeholders can build trust with consumers and regulators, which is crucial for the long-term success of the industry.

Furthermore, stakeholders in the AI ecosystem should actively engage with policymakers and regulators to shape the regulatory landscape in a way that fosters innovation while also protecting the rights and interests of individuals. By participating in the policymaking process, stakeholders can help in creating a conducive environment for AI development and deployment.

Lastly, it is important for stakeholders to collaborate with each other and share knowledge and resources for the greater good of the industry. By working together, stakeholders can leverage each other's strengths and expertise, leading to more impactful and sustainable outcomes. Overall, by following these recommendations, stakeholders in the AI ecosystem can contribute to the continued growth and success of the industry on a global scale.